Contents

1 Chapter 1: Fiscal Policy Foundations

Fiscal policy, at its core, represents the strategic use of government spending and taxation to influence a nation's economic trajectory. It's a powerful lever, capable of stimulating growth during downturns or tempering inflation when the economy overheats. Understanding its foundations is crucial for anyone seeking to grasp the intricacies of national prosperity. But let's be clear, it is not a magic wand; effective implementation requires a nuanced understanding of economic principles and a keen awareness of potential consequences.

Governments wield two primary tools within the fiscal policy arsenal: spending and taxation. Government spending encompasses a wide array of expenditures, from infrastructure projects and education initiatives to social welfare programs and national defense. These investments inject money directly into the economy, creating jobs, boosting demand, and fostering economic activity. Think of it as priming the pump – a deliberate effort to kickstart a sluggish engine. Taxation, on the other hand, involves the collection of revenue from individuals and businesses. Taxes fund government programs, reduce disposable income, and can influence economic behavior. For example, higher taxes on luxury goods might curb consumption, while tax incentives for renewable energy could encourage investment in green technologies. Striking the right balance between spending and taxation is the key to achieving desired economic outcomes.

Different schools of thought offer contrasting perspectives on the optimal approach to fiscal policy. Keynesian economics, for instance, advocates for active government intervention to stabilize the economy, particularly during recessions. According to this view, governments should increase spending and cut taxes to boost aggregate demand and stimulate economic growth. Conversely, supply-side economics emphasizes the importance of tax cuts and deregulation to incentivize investment, production, and job creation. Proponents of this approach argue that lower taxes will ultimately lead to greater economic activity and higher overall tax revenues. These are just two prominent examples, and the debate over the most effective fiscal policy continues to evolve.

The interplay between fiscal and monetary policy is essential to comprehend. Monetary policy, managed by central banks, primarily focuses on controlling interest rates and the money supply to influence inflation and economic growth. While fiscal policy directly impacts aggregate demand through government spending and taxation, monetary policy works indirectly by influencing borrowing costs and investment decisions. When coordinated effectively, fiscal and monetary policies can create a stable and predictable economic environment. For instance, during a recession, a government might implement expansionary fiscal policies (increased spending, lower taxes) while the central bank lowers interest rates to further stimulate the economy. However, conflicting policies can undermine each other, leading to uncertainty and instability.

Budgeting approaches are as diverse as the nations that employ them. Traditional budgeting, often based on incremental changes to previous budgets, provides stability but can perpetuate inefficiencies. Performance-based budgeting, on the other hand, links funding to specific outcomes and performance metrics, promoting accountability and efficiency. Zero-based budgeting requires each department to justify its entire budget from scratch every year, forcing a thorough evaluation of all programs and activities. Each approach has its strengths and weaknesses, and the choice depends on the specific goals and priorities of the government.

Furthermore, understanding the potential pitfalls of fiscal policy is just as crucial as grasping its potential benefits. Excessive government spending can lead to inflation, crowding out private investment, and accumulating unsustainable levels of debt. High taxes can discourage work, savings, and investment, hindering economic growth. Political considerations can also influence fiscal policy decisions, leading to inefficient or even counterproductive outcomes. A well-designed fiscal policy must be based on sound economic principles, carefully consider potential consequences, and be insulated from undue political influence.

To illustrate these concepts, let's consider a hypothetical scenario. Imagine a country facing a prolonged economic recession with rising unemployment and declining consumer confidence. Following a Keynesian approach, the government might decide to implement a stimulus package that includes increased spending on infrastructure projects, such as building new roads and bridges, and temporary tax cuts for lower-income households. These measures would inject money directly into the economy, creating jobs, boosting demand, and stimulating economic activity. Meanwhile, the central bank might lower interest rates to encourage borrowing and investment. If implemented effectively, these coordinated policies could help the country emerge from the recession and return to a path of sustainable growth.

Fiscal policy decisions have long-term consequences that extend far beyond the immediate economic impact. Government spending on education, research and development, and infrastructure can boost productivity, innovation, and long-term economic growth. Social welfare programs can reduce poverty and inequality, creating a more inclusive and equitable society. National defense spending can protect national security and promote stability. But these investments must be carefully planned and managed to ensure that they generate maximum benefits for future generations.

Ultimately, effective fiscal policy requires a commitment to sound economic principles, a long-term perspective, and a willingness to make difficult choices. It's about balancing competing priorities, weighing potential benefits and risks, and ensuring that government budgets are aligned with national goals and values. It's a complex and challenging task, but one that is essential for building a prosperous and sustainable future.

2 Chapter 2: Revenue Mobilization Strategies

Effective revenue mobilization is the lifeblood of any nation striving for prosperity. It's more than just collecting taxes; it's about strategically designing and implementing a system that fuels economic growth, supports essential public services, and ensures a stable fiscal future. For a beginner navigating this complex terrain, understanding the diverse strategies available and their practical application is paramount. We will dissect the primary avenues for revenue generation and provide actionable insights into optimizing each.

Taxation, the cornerstone of government revenue, demands a nuanced approach. Income tax, whether levied on individuals or corporations, needs to be calibrated to incentivize productivity and investment. A progressive income tax system, where higher earners pay a larger percentage of their income, can promote social equity and fund vital social programs, but it also runs the risk of discouraging high-income earners and businesses from operating within the country. Balancing these competing considerations requires a deep understanding of the local economic context and careful modeling of the potential effects of tax rate changes. VAT, or Value Added Tax, offers a broad-based consumption tax that can generate substantial revenue. Its relative simplicity and self-policing mechanism (businesses have an incentive to claim input credits, thus ensuring that VAT is collected at each stage of the production process) make it an attractive option for many countries. However, it can disproportionately affect low-income households, who spend a larger percentage of their income on consumption. Mitigating this requires careful consideration of exemptions for essential goods and services or implementing targeted social safety nets. Excise duties, taxes on specific goods such as alcohol, tobacco, and fuel, serve a dual purpose: revenue generation and discouraging consumption of harmful products. These taxes can be politically palatable, as they are often seen as targeting "sinful" activities. However, they can also be regressive and may lead to smuggling or the development of black markets if set too high. A comprehensive tax strategy therefore demands an integrated assessment of these different tax instruments, tailored to a nation's specific economic and social goals.

Beyond taxation, non-tax revenue sources offer a crucial supplementary stream. Royalties, derived from the extraction of natural resources, can contribute significantly to government coffers, especially in resource-rich countries. Negotiating favorable royalty agreements with mining companies and other extractive industries is critical. Fees and charges, levied for specific government services such as licenses, permits, and user fees for public facilities, provide a direct link between service provision and revenue generation. These should be set at levels that reflect the cost of providing the service and avoid creating undue barriers to access. Investment income, generated from government investments in stocks, bonds, and other financial assets, can also provide a valuable revenue stream. Prudent management of these investments is crucial to maximize returns and minimize risk. Furthermore, governments can explore revenue generation through privatization of state-owned enterprises or by leasing out public assets. Effectively leveraging these non-tax revenue streams requires careful management, transparent accounting, and robust regulatory frameworks to prevent corruption and ensure that the benefits accrue to the nation as a whole.

Broadening the tax base is a cornerstone of sustainable revenue mobilization. This involves bringing more individuals and businesses into the formal tax system, thereby increasing the overall pool of taxable income and economic activity. Simplifying tax laws and procedures is crucial to make it easier for taxpayers to comply. This includes reducing the number of tax brackets, streamlining filing processes, and providing clear and accessible information about tax obligations. Strengthening tax administration is equally important. This involves investing in technology and training to improve tax collection efficiency, detect and prevent tax evasion, and enhance taxpayer service. Initiatives such as automated tax filing systems, data analytics to identify potential tax cheats, and improved customer service can significantly boost tax compliance. Additionally, combating the informal economy, where economic activity goes unreported and untaxed, is essential. This can involve offering incentives for businesses to formalize, cracking down on illegal activities, and promoting financial inclusion to bring more individuals into the formal banking system.

Combating tax evasion and avoidance is paramount to ensuring a fair and efficient tax system. Aggressive tax planning and outright tax evasion can significantly erode the tax base and undermine public finances. Strengthening tax laws to close loopholes and address aggressive tax avoidance strategies is crucial. This includes implementing measures to prevent profit shifting by multinational corporations, tightening rules on tax havens, and increasing penalties for tax evasion. Enhancing international cooperation on tax matters is also essential. This involves sharing information with other countries to combat cross-border tax evasion and participating in international initiatives to combat tax avoidance by multinational corporations. Investing in specialized units within tax administrations to investigate and prosecute tax evaders can also send a strong deterrent signal. Public awareness campaigns can also help to promote tax compliance by educating taxpayers about their obligations and the importance of paying taxes to fund public services.

Effective tax administration is the linchpin of successful revenue mobilization. A modern and efficient tax administration can significantly improve tax compliance and reduce tax evasion. Investing in technology is essential. This includes implementing integrated tax administration systems that automate key processes such as tax filing, payment processing, and audit selection. Data analytics can also be used to identify potential tax cheats and improve the efficiency of tax audits.

Training and capacity building for tax officials is equally important. This includes providing tax officials with the skills and knowledge they need to effectively administer the tax laws and detect and prevent tax evasion. Improving taxpayer service is also crucial. This involves providing taxpayers with clear and accessible information about their tax obligations, making it easy for them to file and pay their taxes, and resolving disputes fairly and efficiently. A taxpayer-friendly tax administration can significantly improve tax compliance and build trust in the tax system.

Ultimately, successful revenue mobilization requires a holistic approach that considers the interplay between different revenue sources, the need for a fair and efficient tax system, and the importance of good governance and transparency. It is not merely about maximizing revenue collection; it is about creating a fiscal environment that supports sustainable economic growth, promotes social equity, and enhances national prosperity. Regularly evaluating and adapting revenue mobilization strategies to changing economic conditions and policy priorities is essential to ensure their continued effectiveness. Moreover, engaging with stakeholders, including businesses, civil society organizations, and the public, in the design and implementation of revenue policies can foster greater buy-in and improve compliance. For beginners, a continuous learning approach, coupled with a commitment to ethical principles and a focus on long-term sustainability, will be key to navigating the complexities of revenue mobilization and contributing to a nation's fiscal well-being.

3 Chapter 3: Expenditure Management Principles

Effective expenditure management is the cornerstone of a well-functioning government, a critical component in transforming ambitious policy goals into tangible improvements for citizens. It's not just about cutting costs; it's about strategically allocating resources to maximize impact and ensure that every taxpayer dollar is used wisely, contributing to national prosperity. This requires a shift from simply tracking spending to actively managing it with a clear focus on achieving desired outcomes. As a responsible government, one must embrace principles that promote efficiency, effectiveness, and accountability in all spending decisions.

One of the cardinal principles of sound expenditure management is value for money. This goes beyond simply selecting the lowest bidder. It entails a comprehensive assessment of the total cost of ownership, considering factors like quality, durability, maintenance, and long-term benefits. For instance, when procuring infrastructure projects, governments shouldn't just focus on the initial construction cost but also consider the long-term maintenance expenses and the project's expected lifespan. A slightly more expensive option that offers superior quality and durability may ultimately provide better value for money in the long run. It demands that every expenditure decision is justified by a thorough cost-benefit analysis, ensuring that resources are allocated to projects and programs that deliver the greatest possible return on investment for the nation.

Efficiency is another crucial principle. It involves optimizing processes and eliminating waste to minimize the cost of delivering public services. This could involve streamlining bureaucratic procedures, adopting technology to automate tasks, or renegotiating contracts with suppliers. Lean management techniques, often used in the private sector, can be adapted to the public sector to identify and eliminate inefficiencies in government operations. For example, transitioning from paper-based systems to digital platforms can significantly reduce administrative costs and improve service delivery speed. Investing in staff training and development is also essential to enhance efficiency, as skilled and knowledgeable employees are better equipped to identify and implement improvements in their work processes. Remember, every dollar saved through increased efficiency can be redirected to other pressing needs, boosting overall government effectiveness.

Effectiveness, closely linked to efficiency, focuses on achieving desired policy outcomes. It's not enough to simply spend money; the spending must actually lead to the intended results. This requires clearly defining objectives, setting measurable targets, and regularly monitoring progress. For example, if the government invests in education programs aimed at improving literacy rates, it needs to track literacy rates before and after the program implementation to assess its effectiveness. Regular evaluations are essential to identify what works and what doesn't, allowing for adjustments to programs and policies to improve their impact. A commitment to evidence-based policymaking is crucial, ensuring that decisions are informed by data and rigorous analysis rather than political considerations or outdated assumptions.

Prioritization is an inevitable aspect of expenditure management. Governments face competing demands for limited resources, so it's essential to establish clear priorities and allocate funds accordingly. This requires a strategic planning process that identifies the most pressing needs and aligns spending with national development goals. Sectoral priorities, as will be discussed later, must be carefully considered in light of their potential contribution to economic growth, social equity, and environmental sustainability. For example, a government facing high unemployment might prioritize investments in job creation programs and infrastructure projects that stimulate economic activity. Transparent decision-making processes are crucial to ensure that prioritization is fair and equitable, taking into account the needs of all stakeholders.

Cost control is an ongoing imperative, requiring vigilance and discipline throughout the budget cycle. This involves establishing clear spending limits, monitoring expenditure closely, and taking corrective action when necessary. Budget overruns can undermine fiscal stability and erode public trust, so it's essential to have robust mechanisms in place to prevent them. This may involve strengthening financial management systems, improving procurement practices, and holding departments accountable for staying within their allocated budgets. Regular audits are essential to identify instances of waste, fraud, and abuse, and to ensure that public funds are used appropriately. It's not about stifling innovation or cutting essential services; it's about ensuring that every dollar is spent wisely and effectively.

Financial administration plays a crucial role in ensuring that public funds are spent responsibly and in accordance with legal and regulatory frameworks. This involves establishing sound accounting practices, maintaining accurate financial records, and ensuring compliance with all applicable laws and regulations. Strong internal controls are essential to prevent fraud and corruption. A well-functioning financial administration system is also crucial for producing reliable financial reports that provide accurate information about government finances to policymakers and the public. Investing in the capacity building of financial administrators is essential to ensure they have the skills and knowledge needed to effectively manage public funds.

The principles outlined above are interconnected and mutually reinforcing. Effective expenditure management requires a holistic approach that integrates these principles into all aspects of the budgeting process. It's not a one-time fix but an ongoing commitment to continuous improvement. Governments that embrace these principles will be better equipped to allocate resources efficiently, achieve desired policy outcomes, and ultimately contribute to the prosperity of their nations. The impact of prudent spending resonates across generations, fostering economic stability, social progress, and a brighter future for all. This proactive approach not only safeguards public resources but also builds confidence in the government's ability to effectively manage the nation's finances, reinforcing the foundation for sustainable growth and development. The path to national prosperity is paved with thoughtful planning, disciplined execution, and a steadfast commitment to responsible financial stewardship.

4 Chapter 4: Debt and Deficit Dynamics

Government deficits and debt are often portrayed as simple numbers, but beneath the surface lies a complex interplay of economic forces. Understanding these dynamics is crucial for navigating the turbulent waters of fiscal policy and ensuring national prosperity. Ignoring them can lead to severe consequences, impacting everything from interest rates to the availability of public services, and ultimately, the economic well-being of citizens. I remember a case where a seemingly small, unchecked deficit spiraled out of control, leading to a period of austerity that significantly hampered economic growth and eroded public trust. This is why dissecting the causes, consequences, and management strategies of government debt and deficits is so important.

Budget deficits, occurring when government spending exceeds revenue within a fiscal year, can arise from various sources. Recessions are a prime culprit, as economic downturns lead to decreased tax revenues and increased demand for social safety nets like unemployment benefits. Expansionary fiscal policies, often employed to stimulate a sluggish economy, can also contribute to deficits if spending increases are not offset by corresponding revenue gains. Furthermore, demographic shifts, such as an aging population, can strain government resources as pension and healthcare costs rise. Think about it this way: a farmer might take out a loan to invest in new equipment, hoping for a larger harvest in the future. Similarly, governments sometimes borrow to finance investments in infrastructure or education, aiming for long-term economic growth. However, just like the farmer needs to manage his debt carefully, governments must exercise prudence in their borrowing decisions.

The consequences of persistent deficits are far-reaching. One immediate effect is increased government borrowing, which can drive up interest rates. Higher interest rates make it more expensive for businesses to invest and consumers to borrow, potentially dampening economic activity. Moreover, large deficits can lead to inflation if the government resorts to printing money to finance its spending. This can erode the purchasing power of individuals and businesses, creating economic instability. Perhaps the most concerning consequence is the accumulation of government debt, which represents the total amount of money owed by the government to its creditors. As debt grows, the government must allocate a larger portion of its budget to debt service, diverting resources from essential public services like education, healthcare, and infrastructure. I have seen firsthand how crippling debt can force governments to make difficult choices, sacrificing long-term investments for short-term fiscal stability.

Effective debt management is therefore paramount. Governments can employ several strategies to mitigate the risks associated with high debt levels. One approach is debt refinancing, where existing debt is replaced with new debt at a lower interest rate or with more favorable terms. This can reduce the government's debt service burden and free up resources for other priorities. Another strategy is debt restructuring, which involves renegotiating the terms of existing debt with creditors. This might include extending the repayment period, reducing the interest rate, or even writing off a portion of the debt. Fiscal consolidation, a set of policies designed to reduce government deficits and debt, is also crucial. This can involve raising taxes, cutting spending, or a combination of both. The key is to implement these measures in a way that minimizes the negative impact on economic growth and social welfare. The relationship between debt and economic growth is a complex and hotly debated topic. Some economists argue that moderate levels of government debt can be beneficial, as they allow governments to finance investments that boost long-term economic growth. Others contend that high levels of debt can stifle growth by crowding out private investment, increasing uncertainty, and creating a drag on future generations. The optimal level of government debt is likely to vary depending on a country's specific circumstances, including its economic structure, institutional framework, and demographic profile. What is sustainable for one country may be unsustainable for another. Ultimately, the key is to ensure that government debt is used to finance productive investments that generate long-term economic benefits. I firmly believe that a well-managed debt, channeled towards strategic sectors, can act as a catalyst for sustainable development.

Assessing the sustainability of government debt requires a comprehensive analysis of various factors. The debt-to-GDP ratio, which measures government debt as a percentage of gross domestic product, is a widely used indicator of debt sustainability. A high debt-to-GDP ratio can signal that a country is struggling to manage its debt burden and may be at risk of default. However, this ratio alone is not sufficient to determine debt sustainability. Other factors, such as the country's economic growth rate, interest rates, and primary fiscal balance (the difference between government revenue and spending excluding interest payments), must also be considered. A country with a strong economic growth rate and a healthy primary fiscal balance is better positioned to manage its debt than a country with weak growth and a large primary deficit.

The impact of a high debt-to-GDP ratio on national prosperity can be significant. As mentioned earlier, high debt levels can lead to higher interest rates, reduced investment, and inflation. They can also erode investor confidence, leading to capital flight and currency depreciation. This can further exacerbate the debt burden and create a vicious cycle of economic decline. Moreover, high debt levels can constrain the government's ability to respond to economic shocks, such as recessions or natural disasters. This can leave the country vulnerable to economic instability and hinder its ability to achieve its development goals. Therefore, maintaining a sustainable level of government debt is essential for ensuring long-term national prosperity.

In conclusion, navigating the intricate landscape of debt and deficit dynamics demands a nuanced understanding of their causes, consequences, and management strategies. Prudent fiscal policy, coupled with effective debt management, is crucial for safeguarding national prosperity and ensuring a sustainable future for generations to come. Governments must prioritize investments that promote long-term economic growth, maintain fiscal discipline, and ensure transparency and accountability in the budgeting process. By doing so, they can harness the power of fiscal policy to build a more prosperous and equitable society. It's not just about balancing the books; it's about investing in a better future.

5 Chapter 5: Budget Transparency and Accountability

Budget transparency isn't just about making documents available online; it's about fostering a culture of openness that allows citizens to understand, scrutinize, and participate in government financial decisions. Think of it as sunlight disinfecting a wound – the more light shone on the process, the less likely corruption and mismanagement can fester. For a beginner, understanding the basic tenets of budget transparency is your first step towards holding your government accountable. This starts with knowing where to find the information. Most governments, at least in theory, publish budget documents online. These documents range from the executive budget proposal to enacted budgets, audit reports, and performance evaluations. Learning how to navigate these resources – often complex and jargon-laden – is a crucial skill. Look for summaries, plain language explanations, or even citizen-friendly budget guides created by NGOs or civic groups. Don't be intimidated by the technical language; focus on understanding the big picture – where is the money coming from, and where is it going?

Accountability, in turn, is the mechanism that ensures transparency translates into responsible governance. Without accountability, transparency is merely window dressing. It is a multi-faceted concept. Financial accountability ensures funds are used for their intended purposes and in compliance with regulations. Performance accountability assesses whether government programs are achieving their stated goals and delivering value for money. Political accountability holds elected officials responsible for their budget decisions. A key tool for fostering accountability is independent audit. Audit reports, ideally conducted by independent bodies, can reveal irregularities, inefficiencies, and even outright fraud. Pay attention to audit findings and recommendations, and demand that your elected officials take action to address any issues identified. Legislative oversight also plays a crucial role. Parliamentary committees should scrutinize budget proposals, monitor budget execution, and hold government officials accountable for their spending decisions.

To truly engage with the budget process, learn to analyze budget documents beyond just finding them. Look for trends. How has government spending changed over time? Which sectors are receiving increased or decreased funding? Are these changes aligned with national priorities and economic realities? Compare budgeted amounts with actual expenditures. Significant discrepancies could indicate overspending, underspending, or poor budget planning. Analyze the allocation of resources across different programs and projects. Are resources being directed towards the most effective and impactful initiatives? Look for evidence of waste, duplication, or inefficient spending. All governments make difficult choices when allocating scarce resources. Understanding the trade-offs involved is crucial for informed citizen participation.

Citizen participation is not just about attending town hall meetings, although those can be valuable. It's about using the information you gain from budget documents to engage in meaningful dialogue with government officials, advocating for your priorities, and demanding accountability. Write to your elected representatives, participate in online forums, and support organizations that advocate for budget transparency and accountability. A powerful tool is to track the performance of government programs. Are schools improving? Are hospitals providing better care? Are roads being maintained? Use this information to hold your government accountable for delivering results. Social media can also be a powerful tool for promoting budget transparency and accountability. Use it to share information, raise awareness, and mobilize public opinion. However, be sure to verify information before sharing it, and avoid spreading misinformation.

Remember that corruption thrives in darkness. By demanding budget transparency and accountability, you can help to shine a light on government finances and reduce the opportunities for corruption. Report suspected cases of corruption to the appropriate authorities, and support efforts to strengthen anti-corruption measures. Whistleblower protection laws are essential for encouraging people to come forward with information about corruption. However, even with the best laws, it takes courage to speak out. Support whistleblowers and advocate for stronger protections for them.

A fundamental element of budget transparency is ensuring that the information presented is accessible and understandable to the average citizen. This goes beyond simply publishing documents online. Governments should strive to present budget information in a clear, concise, and user-friendly manner, using visualizations, infographics, and plain language explanations. They should also actively engage with citizens to explain budget priorities and address their concerns. Public consultations and participatory budgeting initiatives can be valuable tools for engaging citizens in the budget process. Participatory budgeting allows citizens to directly decide how a portion of the public budget is spent. This can empower citizens, improve the quality of public services, and increase trust in government.

Building a culture of transparency and accountability takes time and effort. It requires a commitment from both government officials and citizens. But the rewards are significant: a more efficient, effective, and accountable government that serves the interests of all its citizens. Start small. Focus on understanding the basics of budget transparency and accountability, and then gradually expand your knowledge and engagement. Don't be afraid to ask questions, challenge assumptions, and demand answers. Your voice matters.

As you delve deeper, explore the role of technology in enhancing budget transparency. Open data initiatives can make budget information more accessible and usable. Data visualization tools can help citizens to understand complex budget data. Online platforms can facilitate citizen engagement and feedback. These tools can help to empower citizens, improve the quality of public services, and increase trust in government. However, technology is not a panacea. It is important to ensure that technology is used in a way that is equitable, inclusive, and accessible to all citizens. For example, efforts should be made to bridge the digital divide and ensure that everyone has access to the internet and the skills to use it effectively.

Finally, remember that budget transparency and accountability are not just technical issues; they are fundamental to good governance and democratic participation. They are essential for ensuring that government resources are used effectively and efficiently, and that citizens have a voice in how their government is run. By demanding budget transparency and accountability, you can help to build a stronger, more prosperous, and more just society. Embrace the challenge, stay informed, and hold your government accountable. The future of your nation depends on it. The journey to fiscal responsibility starts with a single step – your informed participation.

6 Chapter 6: Sectoral Budgeting Priorities

Sectoral budgeting priorities are essentially the roadmap for how a nation invests in its future. Instead of viewing the budget as a monolithic entity, dissecting it sector by sector reveals the true character of a government's policy objectives and its commitment to various aspects of national prosperity. Understanding these priorities requires a nuanced appreciation of the interplay between economic growth, social equity, and strategic imperatives. Think of it as baking a cake; you need the right ingredients in the right proportions to achieve the desired outcome. In our case, these ingredients are the financial resources allocated to education, healthcare, infrastructure, defense, and other critical sectors.

The allocation of budget resources across sectors is far from arbitrary; it should ideally reflect a nation's strategic goals, developmental needs, and societal values. Consider, for instance, a developing nation aiming to transition from an agrarian economy to a manufacturing hub. In such a scenario, a significant portion of the budget might be directed toward infrastructure development (roads, ports, energy) and education, particularly technical and vocational training. Conversely, a nation grappling with an aging population might prioritize healthcare spending and social security programs. It's not just about spending more; it's about spending smarter, channeling resources to where they will have the greatest impact on long-term prosperity. This is why understanding the rationale behind these priorities is paramount. Economic development hinges on a skilled workforce, robust infrastructure, and a stable political environment, all of which require careful and strategic investment.

One of the most pressing challenges in sectoral budgeting is balancing competing demands. Every sector has its advocates, each vying for a larger slice of the pie. The education lobby might argue that increased funding for schools and universities is essential for fostering innovation and competitiveness. The healthcare sector might emphasize the urgent need for investments in hospitals, medical research, and disease prevention. The defense establishment might highlight the importance of maintaining a strong military for national security. Reconciling these competing demands requires a transparent and evidence-based decision-making process. Policymakers must weigh the costs and benefits of each allocation, considering the potential impact on economic growth, social equity, and national security. For example, while increased defense spending might enhance national security, it could also divert resources away from education and healthcare, potentially hindering long-term economic development. It is crucial, therefore, to strike a delicate balance, ensuring that each sector receives adequate funding without jeopardizing the overall fiscal health of the nation.

To evaluate the effectiveness of sectoral budget allocations, we need to look beyond mere expenditure figures. We must delve into the outcomes achieved with those resources. Key performance indicators (KPIs) play a crucial role in assessing the impact of budget allocations on various sectors. In education, for instance, we might track student enrollment rates, literacy levels, graduation rates, and the performance of students on standardized tests. In healthcare, we might monitor life expectancy, infant mortality rates, disease prevalence, and access to medical services. In infrastructure, we might assess the quality of roads, the reliability of energy supply, and the efficiency of transportation networks. By tracking these indicators over time, policymakers can gain valuable insights into the effectiveness of their budgeting decisions and identify areas where improvements are needed. For instance, if a nation significantly increases its investment in education but sees little improvement in literacy rates, it might be necessary to re-evaluate its education policies and programs. The budget itself is not a static document, but rather a dynamic instrument that should adapt to changing circumstances and evolving priorities.

Furthermore, sectoral budgeting priorities should be aligned with a nation's long-term strategic goals. If a country aspires to become a leader in renewable energy, it should allocate sufficient resources to research and development, infrastructure development, and workforce training in this sector. Similarly, if a nation aims to reduce income inequality, it should prioritize investments in education, healthcare, and social welfare programs targeted at disadvantaged communities. The budget should not merely reflect the current state of affairs but should also serve as a catalyst for achieving future aspirations. This requires a long-term perspective and a commitment to strategic planning.

However, it's important to acknowledge that sectoral budgeting is not an exact science. It involves inherent uncertainties and trade-offs. Economic forecasts can be inaccurate, unforeseen events (such as natural disasters or global pandemics) can disrupt budget plans, and political considerations can influence resource allocation decisions. Nevertheless, by adopting a transparent, evidence-based, and strategic approach, nations can maximize the effectiveness of their sectoral budgeting priorities and pave the way for sustained national prosperity.

To make this clearer, I would like to talk about a personal experience. I remember advising a small developing nation on its budget allocation process. They were heavily reliant on agriculture, but their productivity was low, and their infrastructure was dilapidated. After a thorough analysis, we recommended a shift in sectoral priorities, focusing on infrastructure development (irrigation systems, rural roads) and agricultural extension services (training farmers in modern techniques). Initially, there was resistance from some quarters, who argued that these investments would take time to yield results. However, within a few years, we saw a significant increase in agricultural productivity, which led to higher incomes for farmers and a boost to the national economy. This experience underscored the importance of making strategic and informed decisions, even when they are not immediately popular.

In conclusion, understanding sectoral budgeting priorities is crucial for anyone interested in national prosperity. It's about understanding how a nation invests in its future, the rationale behind those investments, and the mechanisms for evaluating their effectiveness. By adopting a transparent, evidence-based, and strategic approach, policymakers can ensure that budget resources are allocated in a way that maximizes economic growth, social equity, and national security. Only then can we truly orchestrate government budgets for sustained and inclusive prosperity. Remember, every line item in the budget represents a choice, a priority, and a commitment to a particular vision of the future. And it is up to us to ensure that these choices are made wisely and in the best interests of the nation.

7 Chapter 7: Future Trends in Public Finance

The world of public finance isn't static; it's a constantly shifting landscape influenced by technological advancements, evolving global dynamics, and changing societal priorities. Understanding these emerging trends is crucial for policymakers, financial professionals, and even informed citizens who want to ensure a prosperous and sustainable future for their nations. Therefore, let's explore some of the pivotal forces shaping the future of how governments manage their budgets and resources.

One of the most significant shifts we're witnessing is the increasing digitalization of public services and financial processes. This isn't just about moving paperwork online; it's a fundamental transformation of how governments interact with citizens and manage their internal operations. Consider the potential of blockchain technology to enhance transparency and security in government procurement. By creating an immutable and auditable record of transactions, blockchain can help to reduce corruption and improve accountability. Think, too, of how digital identities can streamline the delivery of social welfare programs, ensuring that benefits reach those who are truly entitled to them while minimizing fraud and administrative costs. The rise of digital currencies, too, presents both opportunities and challenges for public finance. While central bank digital currencies (CBDCs) could potentially reduce transaction costs and improve financial inclusion, they also raise complex questions about privacy, monetary policy, and financial stability. Embracing this technological revolution responsibly will demand careful planning, robust cybersecurity measures, and a commitment to bridging the digital divide to ensure that all citizens can benefit from these advancements.

Globalization, while not a new phenomenon, continues to exert a profound influence on public finance. The interconnectedness of national economies means that fiscal policies in one country can have significant spillover effects on others. This necessitates greater international cooperation and coordination in areas such as tax policy, debt management, and financial regulation. The rise of multinational corporations and global value chains has also created new challenges for tax authorities. It's becoming increasingly difficult to track profits and ensure that companies pay their fair share of taxes in the countries where they operate. Addressing this requires a concerted effort to combat tax avoidance and evasion through international initiatives such as the OECD's Base Erosion and Profit Shifting (BEPS) project. Furthermore, globalization has intensified competition for foreign investment, leading some countries to engage in a "race to the bottom" by lowering corporate tax rates.

This can erode the tax base and undermine the ability of governments to finance essential public services. Finding a balance between attracting investment and maintaining a sustainable level of revenue is a key challenge for policymakers in an increasingly globalized world.

Demographic shifts are also placing considerable strain on public finances in many countries. Aging populations, declining birth rates, and increased life expectancy are leading to a surge in demand for healthcare, pensions, and social care services. At the same time, the shrinking workforce means that there are fewer people to contribute to the tax base. This creates a fiscal squeeze that requires governments to make difficult choices about how to allocate resources. Some countries are exploring reforms to their pension systems, such as raising the retirement age or shifting from defined benefit to defined contribution schemes. Others are focusing on strategies to promote healthy aging and reduce healthcare costs. Encouraging greater labor force participation among older workers and investing in education and training to boost productivity are also crucial steps. Addressing these demographic challenges will require a long-term perspective and a willingness to make unpopular decisions.

Another critical area that will dominate future public finance discussions is sustainability. The growing awareness of climate change and its potential impact on economies and societies is forcing governments to rethink their fiscal policies. Investing in renewable energy, energy efficiency, and sustainable transportation is not just an environmental imperative; it's also an economic one. Governments can use fiscal incentives, such as tax credits and subsidies, to encourage businesses and individuals to adopt more sustainable practices. Carbon pricing mechanisms, such as carbon taxes and cap-and-trade systems, can also play a role in reducing emissions and generating revenue that can be used to finance green investments. Beyond climate change, sustainability also encompasses broader issues such as social equity and economic resilience. Ensuring that all citizens have access to education, healthcare, and other essential services is crucial for creating a more just and equitable society. Investing in infrastructure, innovation, and skills development can help to build a more resilient economy that is better equipped to withstand future shocks.

In conclusion, the future of public finance will be shaped by a complex interplay of technological, global, demographic, and environmental forces. Navigating these challenges successfully will require innovative thinking, sound fiscal management, and a commitment to long-term sustainability. It will also necessitate greater transparency and accountability in government budgeting and spending, as well as increased citizen engagement in the policy-making process. By embracing these principles, governments can ensure that public finances are used to promote national prosperity and create a better future for all. I believe these trends will continue to shape the public finance landscape for the foreseeable future. Adaptability and foresight will be key to navigating these changes effectively and ensuring a financially stable and prosperous future for all nations.

www.ingramcontent.com/pod-product-compliance
Lightning Source LLC
LaVergne TN
LVHW022031200926
848481LV00007B/2642
9798349521577